Who's Who at School

by **Mark Weakland**   illustrated by **Nina de Polonia-Nill**

PICTURE WINDOW BOOKS
a capstone imprint

Mason

Name: **Mason**

Birthday: **April 19**

Favorite color: **red**

Favorite food: **anything spicy**

Favorite animal: **polar bear**

I want to be a: **firefighter**

Table of Contents

Who Works at School?

School is a place full of hardworking people. Some are busy in the office. Others bustle around in classrooms. They do many jobs. They teach. They make food. They help students stay safe and healthy. Everybody who works in a school cares about kids.

Hi, I'm Mason, and this is my school. Come on in! I'll show you who's who.

The Principal

This is the principal of my school. She's in charge of the building. It's a big job. She makes sure teachers and kids have everything they need to learn and be safe. She greets students in the morning. She makes sure the hallways are safe. She reminds us of the school rules. When teachers have questions, she answers them. When parents are troubled, she listens to them.

YOUR TURN! Pretend you're a school principal. What kinds of things would you do to keep your students happy and safe?

Office Helpers

The office coordinators work in the office. They are busy all day long. In the morning, they let everyone into the building. They sign in all parents and visitors who come to the school. They answer phones, set up meetings, and keep track of the lunch orders. Later, they type letters and send out mail and email.

Whew! What a lot of work!

The School Counselor

Meet our school counselor. He's a special person. First, he is a good listener. You can share your feelings with him. He's also a problem solver. And I don't mean math problems! The school counselor helps you feel better when your life is tough. He lends a hand if you're being bullied. He even helps bullies learn from their mistakes.

Special-Subject Teachers

There are lots of cool classroom teachers in my school. They teach us math, English, and science. But we've got special-subject teachers too. We have a gym teacher and a music teacher. We also have teachers who help us with art and extra reading classes. One of *my* favorites is our media specialist! She's awesome. She reads to us and shows us how to find books. She helps us with our makerspace ideas. She knows a lot about computers too.

YOUR TURN! What is your favorite special class and why?

The School Nurse

Do you know how to stay healthy? Our school nurse can teach you. Do you know the best way to wash your hands? Our nurse can tell you. When kids need daily medicine, she makes sure they take it. When I scraped my knee at recess, she put a bandage on it. Our nurse takes great care of everyone at school.

YOUR TURN! How has a school nurse helped you or your friends?

Cooks and Lunchroom Servers

It's lunchtime, and I'm hungry! Good thing cooks and servers have been busy making food for our lunch. Sometimes we get cold food, like sandwiches and salads. Sometimes the food is hot. I like tacos. After lunch, there are lots of dishes and trays to clean and counters to wipe. The custodians help with the clean-up. Come on! I'll introduce them to you.

Custodians

Custodians are busy all day—fixing and cleaning. They fix drippy faucets and burned-out light bulbs. They collect trash. They mop the floors if someone spills. They keep our classrooms and bathrooms clean and shiny. And they take care of the school outside too. They cut the grass and sweep the sidewalks. They shovel snow. If it wasn't for the custodians' hard work, our building would be a mess!

Taking Care of You and Me

Aren't the people in my school awesome? Each day they work to make sure everything and everyone is taken care of. They teach, cook, answer phones, and mow the grass. They even make us feel good. I'm glad you got to meet these special people. Now tell me all about the special people at *your* school!

YOUR TURN! If you could work one job in your school, what would you do? Would you be the principal? A teacher? A custodian? Why would you choose that job?

Glossary

bustle—to move with great energy

coordinator—someone who makes sure things are in order and running smoothly

counselor—a person who is trained to help with problems and give advice

custodian—a person whose job it is to clean and take care of a building

faucet—an object with a valve that is used to control the flow of water

media specialist—a person who is trained in library science and helps library visitors; also called a librarian

medicine—a pill or other substance used to treat an illness

principal—the head of a public school

Read More

Hopkins, Lee Bennett. *School People.* Honesdale, Penn.: WordSong, 2018.

Manley, Erika S. *Custodians.* Community Helpers. Minneapolis: Jump!, Inc., 2018.

Smith, Penny. *A School Like Mine: A Celebration of Schools Around the World.* Children Just Like Me. New York: DK Publishing, 2016.

Internet Sites

Use FactHound to find Internet sites related to this book.

Visit *www.facthound.com*

Just type in 9781515838524 and go.

Critical Thinking Questions

1. The author says, "Everybody who works in a school cares about kids." What evidence does he give to support this statement? Use words and phrases from the text, as well as illustrations, in your answer.

2. Describe what you think would happen if a school didn't have a principal. What if it didn't have office helpers, custodians, or cooks?

3. In this book, the author describes the people who work in a school. Think about your own school. Did the author forget anyone? If so, who?

Index

Look for all the books in the series:

Special thanks to our adviser, Sara Hjelmeland, M.Ed., Kindergarten Teacher, for her expertise.

Editor: Jill Kalz
Designer: Lori Bye
Production Specialist: Laura Manthe
The illustrations in this book were created digitally.

Picture Window Books are published by Capstone
1710 Roe Crest Drive, North Mankato, Minnesota 56003
www.mycapstone.com

Library of Congress Cataloging-in-Publication Data is available on the Library of Congress website.
ISBN 978-1-5158-3852-4 (library binding)
ISBN 978-1-5158-4067-1 (paperback)
ISBN 978-1-5158-3858-6 (eBook PDF)
Summary: Who will I meet at school? All the people inside the cheerfully illustrated *Who's Who at School* care about kids, from the principal to the music teacher, the school nurse to the cooks and custodians. A 1st-person student narrator introduces young readers to common members of a diverse elementary-school community and explains the work they do.

Shutterstock: jannoon028, (notebook) design element throughout

Printed in China.
966